Love Yourself to Life
#Love2Life
Dr. Monica DeBro

Karen,
Don't wait for permission to love yourself fully. You deserve to love yourself. Now.

Dr. Monica DeBro

LOVE YOURSELF TO LIFE

Copyright © 2018 by Monica DeBro

PUBLISHED BY FOREVER SHALOM, LLC

All rights reserved. No part of this book may be reproduced or transmitted in any form or by any means without written permission from the author.

Unless otherwise indicated, all Scripture quotations are taken from the Holy Bible, New Living Translation, copyright © 1996, 2004, 2007 by Tyndale House Foundation. Used by permission of Tyndale House Publishers, Inc., Carol Stream, Illinois 60188. All rights reserved.

Scripture quotations are from The ESV® Bible (The Holy Bible, English Standard Version®), Copyright © 2001 by Crossway, a publishing ministry of Good News Publishers. Used by permission. All rights reserved.

Scripture quotations marked AMP are taken from the Amplified® Bible, Copyright © 1954, 1958, 1962, 1964, 1965, 1987 by The Lockman Foundation. Used by permission.

Scripture quotations marked MSG are taken from The Message. Copyright 1993, 1994, 1995, 1996, 2000, 2001, 2002. Used by permission of NavPress Publishing Group.

Scripture quotations marked KJV are taken from the Holy Bible, King James Version (Public Domain)

Taken from the HOLY BIBLE: EASY-TO-READ VERSION © 2001 by World Bible Translation Center, Inc. and used by permission.

ISBN 978-0-9862890-2-6

978-0-9862890-3-3 (Electronic Version)

Editing by: Darrian Tanner
Cover by: Riddick Agency
Back Cover Photo: Casey Perry Photography
Printed in the United States of America

DEDICATION

This book is dedicated to my parents, Rev. Walter L. DeBro, Sr. and Mrs. Pearlie DeBro. Thank you for being the best parents I could ask for, and thanks for never giving up on me. I am blessed to be your daughter! #Love2Life

Pearlie M. DeBro
(February 14, 1932 – September 1, 2012)

Rev. Walter L. DeBro
(October 26, 1927 – November 7, 2012)

ACKNOWLEGEMENTS

Thank you to my sons, David DeBro and Ovell Scott and my nephew Solomon Harris for always encouraging me and supporting my many endeavors. I look forward to everything that you will accomplish with your God-given talents. You mean more to me than you can ever imagine. To my amazing sisters Laura DeBro-Carter and Ruth Carla DeBro and niece Gwendolyn Carter, it is absolutely fun doing life with you all. Thank you for your support and hilarious text messages.

Marie-Eve Thomas, thank you for being my prayer warrior and sister-friend. You are a blessing in my life, and I love the moments we share and that with a simple look, we can laugh and know exactly what each other is thinking. Deborah Boone, thank you for the cards that give me the boosts and encouragement I need at just the right time! Elaine Cauley, thank you for being a great supporter and I enjoy learning from and with you.

Thank you to the following Women of God for adding value to Love Yourself to Life: Wanda Artis, Cherry Davis-Cook, Marie-Eve Thomas, Elaine Cauley, Minister Evelyn Gaskin, Malissa Davis, Melinda DeLeon, Estella Smith, Venetia Michael, Danielle Esdale, and Cheree McArn.

Table of Contents

Introduction	9
Spending Quality Time with God	23
Self-Talk	37
Your Surroundings	55
Avoid the Comparison Trap	65
Invest in Yourself	75
Motivation and Purpose	83
Closing Remarks	103

Introduction

To acquire wisdom is to love oneself; people who cherish understanding will prosper.

– **Proverbs 19:8**

What is the foundation of **Love Yourself to Life**? What does it mean to **Love Yourself to Life**? The saying "I love you to death" never appealed to me. Why would anyone want to love someone to death? I can grasp "I love you until death do us part." That's different– at least in my viewpoint. As I continued to ponder this concept several years ago, I realized that I didn't want anyone to love me to death but to love me to life. I've almost been loved to death, and it was not a good feeling. It wasn't a good place to be in my life. I was almost loved to death as a result of abusive relationships. I could've been loved to death through a stabbing, but I deflected the knife and was stabbed in the arm. I could've been loved to death on the night I was being choked as the air was being depleted from my lungs. Even to this day, I remember many of the events in which I was almost loved to death, but I do not allow those memories to have a negative impact on my present or future.

When I say 'love you to death', it is not always physical death. When someone is consistently speaking negatively to you and about you, discouraging and preventing you from spending time with family and friends and stopping you from attending church, misusing your finances, and refusing to be there for you emotionally, they are loving you to death. How? You lose sight of who you are, and you are not able to enjoy life as you once did before you trusted the person enough to enter into a relationship with him or her. The concept of loving yourself to life allows you to be present in receiving love and support from others.

The basis of **Love Yourself to Life** indicates that we are going to do everything possible to live a fulfilled life without fear, blame, comparing, judging, or allowing others to minimize our God-given Promises.

Love Yourself to Life embraces:

- Spending quality time with God

- Knowing who you are and not allowing others to minimize you

- Finding something every day to motivate you and guide you towards your purpose–not just any purpose (I'm talking about your very own God given purpose. We'll talk about purpose again in another chapter.)

- Identifying the greatness inside of you

- Being aware of your surroundings/environment

- Not comparing yourself to others

Introduction

- Not minimizing who you are because of someone else's insecurities
- that your past cannot be changed and not allowing the past to interfere with your present and future
- Knowing that you are worthy of God's perfect love
- Identifying true love and knowing that it does not involve physical, emotional, mental, spiritual, or financial abuse
- Knowing, Accepting, and Valuing your self-worth

When you love yourself to life, you have a true confidence in who you are and how you should live in this world. You won't be conformed to the patterns of the world or to what society says you should or should not be. You won't give so much attention to what's happening with others around you. You won't minimize your hopes and dreams to make others feel comfortable.

I encourage you to not diminish who you are to make others feel better about themselves. While my lifestyle is comfortable for me, I had to realize that others may think that it is a bit much. Now I don't have a house on the hills or in the mountains. Nor do I drive a car that will make you turn your head and say, "She's got it going on." I am not extravagant, but someone did question various things I do to make myself happy. For example, getting massages, buying fresh flowers for my home, spending quality time alone, and simply clearing out things I don't use to declutter my home are just a few of the things I do for self-care. Although I consider these activities to be minimal, for people who are not used to loving themselves this way, they can feel as if I am "overdoing it". They can think that it's all unnecessary, but my self-care regiment is important to me. I am aware that these are things that place a smile on my face, and they allow me to enjoy the simple things in life. They bring me joy, satisfaction, and comfort. I have to be comfortable in my environment– my home space and my spot. Have you ever decreased your capacity to **Love Yourself to Life** in order to make others feel comfortable? If so, how did you ultimately feel about changing who you were and changing what brought you joy?

In any relationship, whether personal or professional, when you start making changes, you can easily slip into a consistent focus on pleasing the other person and start to neglect yourself. You will stop embracing the things that once brought you joy and happiness. This can cause you to start resenting the other person and having ill-feelings that could've been avoided had you been upfront and honest from the beginning.

To **Love Yourself to Life** indicates that you understand that "No" is a complete sentence. It does not require an explanation. You don't have to give a reason for why you don't want to do something or why you choose to not be involved in specific plans that someone else thinks you need to be involved in. Sometimes as a courtesy, you may give an explanation, but you shouldn't feel obligated to give a reason or make up an excuse for your decision.

There may even be times when you have made plans to hang out with a friend, but you feel tired and need to take time to rest. You may feel as though you are

Introduction

pushing yourself and that you won't be your best when you all do get together. In this instance, how would you respond? Would you push yourself to go out or politely ask your friend if you can reschedule? Your body needs rest, and it is important that you listen to your body when these signals are firing. If you are not able to function physically, you won't be able to function effectively either mentally or emotionally. To function at full capacity, your body must get re-energized through adequate rest.

The premise to **Love Yourself to Life** may seem daunting for some as you may not see, recognize, or understand your true value and potential. The negative self-talk consistently erupts and causes inner turmoil. The past won't go away, and you keep thinking about 'woulda-shoulda-coulda'. You keep reading text messages over and over again which will cause the wound that brought you pain to remain open and never to heal. The same goes with looking at old photos. The message nor the pictures will change. Hit the delete button and move on. The person who sent the text is not sitting around re-reading what he or she wrote. In order to have a refreshed and renewed mind, you have to think forward. Don't use time and energy focusing on negative things of your past. Even if the negative things happened in the past 24 hours, avoid dwelling on things that take the energy from you. Focus on things that bring you life.

Individuals who embrace the concept of **Love Yourself to Life** enjoy spending time alone. They don't wallow in 'I'm lonely'. There is a vast difference in being lonely and being alone. Being alone indicates having the ability to enjoy life solo at your will. Being alone allows one to experience life on his or her own terms. Being alone indicates freedom.

Lonely, on the other hand, as defined by dictionary.com means:

1. affected with, characterized by, or causing a depressing feeling of being alone; lonesome.

2. destitute of sympathetic or friendly companionship, intercourse, support, etc.: a lonely exile.

3. lone; solitary; without company; companionless.

4. remote from places of human habitation; desolate; unfrequented; bleak.

I strongly believe after reading this definition that you are now aware that you are not in a state of loneliness.

I bring up the concept of being alone versus being lonely to bring light to the conversations I've had with single women who have said they are waiting on their "Boaz" before they start enjoying certain aspects of life. They want to wait on a significant other before they start traveling, before they go on that hot air balloon ride, before they take the leap and purchase a home, and before they take that vacation to the beach and just lay out to enjoy the water, sand, and sun. I've heard someone say, "Why go to paradise without a man?" The truth of the matter is that he might be on the island. You want someone who enjoys doing the same things that you enjoy doing.

Introduction

When I tell women that I take myself out on dates, sometimes I get the strangest look and response. I make plans for a variety of things to do so that I am not always doing the same thing over and over (such as going to dinner). I encourage you to look for things to do in your city and surrounding towns. Look for things that interest you as well as those that don't appeal to you. Going places that don't necessarily appeal to you will open you up to new avenues of meeting new people and stepping outside of your current comfort zone. Here's the catch: Don't wait on your friends to be available. There are times that you will have to go at it alone, and that is perfectly fine. No one is going to judge you for taking time to venture out and enjoy your life. It's your life to enjoy. I am hoping that by reading this you will make adjustments and start doing things out of the box in order to experience different facets of life.

The truth of the matter is that if you are single and you don't learn to enjoy being by yourself, you need to think about how you're going to be able to enjoy life with someone else. Do you like yourself enough to spend time alone? Learn to love spending time with yourself by understanding what it means to **Love Yourself to Life.**

In loving myself to life, I had to realize that it's ok to 'sleep in' sometimes. I had to learn that it is perfectly fine to sit on the couch and watch a movie without a computer or book on my lap. I had to become comfortable embracing new roles and relationships. Everything didn't need to be on a stringent schedule as it once was while I was completing my educational goal. I had to learn to relax in order to Love Myself to Life.

When you **Love Yourself to Life** you know exactly who you are, and others' opinions of you won't cause negative reactions. You won't be emotionally moved by what others say about you. You won't be moved by others' desire for you to remain the same and to not excel to the level that you are meant to reach.

Be aware of the labels that others try to attach to you. When someone identifies you as something that you know is not in alignment with who you are, don't allow it to stir up negative feelings inside of you. As it is said, "Don't let it get under your skin." I was once called 'selfish' and 'hypocritical'. For a few minutes I thought about those two words, but then I quickly shook the thoughts out of my head. Neither one of those words describe me. I am a giving person, and the same person you see in public is the same person I am behind closed doors. I don't have the energy to keep up with two personalities.

If your character functions according to the environment that you are in, it shows that you don't truly believe in who you are. Take a self-discovery moment to become fully aware of your likes, dislikes, beliefs, possibilities, strengths, and weaknesses. Knowing where you are is very important because it allows you to see where you can learn and grow.

Be comfortable being 'you' at all times.
Be comfortable being the SAME 'you' at all times.

Introduction

Below are a few qualities that I have identified as characteristics of people who know how to love themselves to life. The description of each quality listed below was written by my friend, Elaine Cauley.

Love Yourself to Life!

1. Self-forgiving: A key to achieving this is to not function or make decisions based on fear. Fear is the catalyst that makes you feel unworthy of forgiveness. Sometimes we mix-up forgiving with being forgiven. Both are healthy and necessary actions to prevent you from carrying unnecessary baggage.

   For God hath not given us the spirit of fear; but of power, and of love, and of a sound mind.
   2 Timothy 1:7 KJV

2. Self-respect: When you have a clear perspective of how God sees you, you will be able to respect yourself. By doing this, you will also subconsciously demonstrate to others how to respect you.

For I know the plans and thoughts that I have for you,' says the Lord, 'plans for peace and well-being and not for disaster, to give you a future and a hope.
Jeremiah 29:11 AMP

3. Self-reflection: This is a great example of when you take time to gauge where you were, where you are and where you want to be!

Introduction

This reflection doesn't indicate a selfish attitude; it just represents a moment that you take time to do a self-assessment because you value YOU!

Test and evaluate yourselves to see whether you are in the faith and living your lives as [committed] believers. Examine yourselves [not me]! Or do you not recognize this about yourselves [by an ongoing experience] that Jesus Christ is in you—unless indeed you fail the test and are rejected as counterfeit?

2 Corinthians 13:5 AMP

4. Self-control: When situations arise and you can control your anger, you can help others. This does not mean that you allow others to use you as a stepping stool or a doormat. Success in this area comes when you don't allow others to cause you to react as if you have no understanding of the impact that losing your temper could cause.

Let nothing be done through strife or vainglory; but in lowliness of mind let each esteem other better than themselves.

Philippians 2:3 KJV

5. Self-confidence: Some people confuse this with having a large ego. This is not necessarily true. I know you're wondering how to tell the difference. If you have an inflated idea of yourself and/or your capabilities with no fruit to support it, then you have a large inflated ego. Confidence is basically the assurance that you will give it your

Introduction

all no matter what happens!

A large ego deceives himself!
For if a man think himself to be something,
when he is nothing, he deceiveth himself.
Galatians 6:3 KJV

Confidence knows who he is in Christ!
I can do all things through Christ which strengtheneth me.
Philippians 4:13 KJV

6. Self-assurance: This reminds me of the saying– my word is my bond (promise). When you value your own word (promise), you make it with the intentions of seeing it all the way to the finish. If you didn't, you wouldn't say it. God had something to say about this too!

Therefore if any man be in Christ, he is a new creature: old things are passed away; behold, all things are become new.
2 Corinthians 5:17 KJV

7. Self-motivated: Imagine an eagle soaring through the sky without the help or encouragement of anything or anyone. When you are able to stir YOURSELF up to take action, you are SELF-MOTIVATED!

> *But you, beloved, build yourselves up on [the foundation of] your most holy faith [continually progress, rise like an edifice higher and higher], pray in the Holy Spirit.*
> **Jude 1:20 AMP**

8. Self-affirmation: This is like a declaration that you make in order to reach a goal. Affirmations are vows that you speak over someone or to yourself. So you will say it and do it by using the innermost part of yourself to confirm it and declare it all the way to the finish line.

> *I shall not die, but live, and declare the works of the Lord.*
> **Psalm 118:17 KJV**

As we look further into the importance of the Love Yourself to Life concept, I encourage you to increase your awareness of your personal thoughts towards yourself. Throughout the book, I will ask you to write about different topics. Each concept will request 8 responses. The number 8 indicates Resurrection and Regeneration and signifies new beginnings. To Love Yourself to Life will require new beginnings, new ways of seeing situations and circumstances, new transformation of thoughts, and a new outlook on life. Eight is our number!

1. What does Love Yourself to Life look like for you?

2. In considering the concept to Love Yourself to Life, how can it change your perspective of how you see yourself?

Introduction

3. What actions can you take today to Love Yourself to Life more?

4. Identify three areas in which you are aware that you are not concentrating on the importance to Love Yourself to Life.

5. In what ways will you begin to "date yourself"? Even if you are married, you need quiet time to yourself.

6. How can you take time for yourself to continue to learn more about you so that you can be the best for someone else?

7. What actions will you take to prevent someone from loving you to death (either spiritually, mentally, emotionally, physically, or financially)?

8. Action: Write out a scripture or quote to help you embrace the essence to **Love Yourself to Life**.

When you **Love Yourself to Life** completely and know who you are, you will know which path to take.

Love Yourself to Life

Chapter 1
Spending Quality Time with God

I love them that love me; and those that seek me early shall find me. (KJV)
I love all who love me. Those who search will surely find me. (NLT)
Proverbs 8:17

What do you do with the first part of your day? Do you allow God to have the first imprints on your heart and mind? Or do you wait until the busyness of the day requires you to call His name? If you allow Him to have the first part of your day, when those unexpected waves come, you won't be easily frustrated because God would have already prepared you. He will help you with any problem or situation that interrupts your day.

I used to constantly say that I was not a morning person. This was my excuse for not getting up early in the morning for devotional time. I would grumble at the thought of getting out of bed before 6:00am. My normal routine was to get up at 6:00am, shower and be out the door for work no later than 6:45am. I wasn't making time for devotion or quiet time to begin my day. I wasn't having quality time to thank God and seek His guidance. Outside of a quick, "Thank you Father for waking me up this morning" prayer, I wasn't getting much prayer time in during the early morning rising hours.

The truth of the matter is that if I had to be at the airport for an early morning flight, I was a morning person. If I had to meet a group for an early bus ride, I was a morning person. Anything that was a leisure pleasure, I was a morning person. Hmm, what did this say about me? I was actually a morning person if I felt that the task was worth me being so.

For quite some time, my devotion time was in the evening hours. I would spend quality time in the prayer room reading my Bible, going through Bible plans, and writing in my prayer journal. When school began, I found myself writing papers at a coffee shop most evenings and on Saturday mornings. Needless to say, my evening devotion time was interrupted. While I did manage to still have prayer time, there wasn't a devoted time.

I learned that it needed to be a planned time just for me and God. But the thought persisted that I just wasn't a morning person. Yet I wondered how I could continue saying this when no matter what time I would go to sleep, I woke up every morning around 4:30am without an alarm clock. However, the idea of getting out of bed before there was a peak of sunlight was not natural for me. My rationale had always been: Why would I get out of the bed when it was still dark outside?

Develop a Realistic Visual Plan

There was a tugging on my heart to begin my day with quiet time and devotion. This thought kept coming up in my Life Coach Sessions, and it

Chapter 1 | Spending Quality Time with God

became one of those 'enough is enough' moments. My Life Coach Crystal Blackwell, owner of Crystal Clear Results Life Coaching, helped me by developing a visual plan for what the morning would look like with me getting up early. We visually set the scene. This is what we came up with:

- Set Pandora to come on at 5:00am through the surround sound that would play in my bedroom.

- Set the alarm on my telephone to an annoying sound and place it in the bathroom so that I would have to get up to turn it off.

- Get the coffee prepared to make in the morning, including having the cup on the counter to prevent any delays.

- Lay out my robe, slippers/socks, or whatever I wanted to slip into before going downstairs the next morning.

- Be in bed by 10:00pm (That's been a work in progress for several years.)

The next morning, I would get up, brush my teeth, wash my face, and go downstairs to make the coffee and start devotion time. The first few days were challenging, but then I started going to bed with excitement because I wanted to know what song God would wake me up to the next morning. Oh yea, let me tell you about Pandora. For whatever reason, the station would not play music at the scheduled time. I adjusted the time back by five minutes, and it still wouldn't come on at the scheduled time. Finally, after I set it for 4:51am, my bedroom was filled with the beauty of God through worship music. However, on the first day I realized that my Life Coach and I had missed one important step in the visual plan...the bathroom. An adjustment was made on the first day! By creating this simple visual plan, I have become accustomed to getting out of bed when it is still dark outside to spend time with God. This may seem quirky and simple, but it helped me because I am a visual and kinesthetic learner. Visualizing my morning from this perspective has enriched my relationship with God, and I stopped making the excuse that I wasn't a morning person.

Realistically, for some, spending quality time with God in the morning may not be the best routine. I've worked night shift at the hospital before and after a 12-hour shift, the body needs rest. Truthfully, how good will your time be if you are fighting to stay awake and not receiving what you are reading in your Bible? Your prayer and meditation time may result in a very long nap. It happened to me many times which is why I adjusted and became accustomed to my devotion time being in the evening. However, your drive home from work can be spent praying a prayer of adoration, thanksgiving, supplication and/or contrition to God. You can pray about His will for your life. You can listen to and sing along with praise and worship songs.

To gain an intimate relationship with God and to be able to hear His voice clearly requires spending time with Him and making necessary adjustments that may initially seem inconvenient to your normal routine. It is an unrealistic expectation to be able to follow His plan when you don't know what it is.

Chapter 1 | Spending Quality Time with God

You have to make yourself available to God to gain wisdom, insight, and understanding. "My sheep listen to my voice; I know them, and they follow me." (John 10:27) "They won't follow a stranger; they will run from him because they don't know his voice." (John 10:5) To know the voice of God, you must spend quality time with Him.

God's Thoughts Toward Us

Loving Yourself to Life involves knowing and BELIEVING what the Father thinks and desires for you. His thoughts are good towards you and not evil. Whenever you find yourself entertaining a negative thought seed placed in your mind, you have to combat it by speaking positive affirmations about yourself.

I am a firm believer of Proverbs 18:21– "The tongue can bring death or life; those who love to talk will reap the consequences." Instead of negative self-talk, speak care and compassion, empowerment and motivation, and power and strength. More importantly, speak what God says about you. I like to speak God's Word over me in first person.

- I am the head (leader) and not the tail (follower). I am above and not beneath. **Deuteronomy 28:13**

- I have God's peace, and it surpasses all understanding. **Philippians 4:7**

- I am more than a conqueror. **Romans 8:37**

- I am holy and unblemished in God's sight. **Ephesians 1:4**

- My needs are met. **Philippians 4:19**

- I can do all things through Christ because He gives me strength. **Philippians 4:13**

- Although I have sinned, I have been forgiven and washed by Christ's blood. **Ephesians 1:7**

- I have a spirit of power, love, and a sound mind. **2 Timothy 1:7**

The Word is filled with scriptures that describe who we are in Christ. We have to make sure to access His Word on a daily basis and study who God says we are in order to combat the negative thoughts that Satan consistently tries to plant in our minds.

What are some negative thoughts that you are plagued with concerning your self-image (inner and outer)? Beside each of the negative thoughts, write down a scripture that is the complete opposite of the negative thought. The scriptures you find are promised to you if you embrace the promises and follow the commands of God. Receive love from the Father to truly **Love Yourself to Life**!

On the morning of Monday, November 20, 2017 I was driving to work and praying. At some point in the prayer, I said:

"I pray that people will see me. I pray that people will accept me and want to

Chapter 1 | Spending Quality Time with God

get to know me."

Instantly, the Lord replied:

"Me too."

I was blown away. That's exactly what the Father wants for us! He wants for us to SEE Him, ACCEPT Him, and GET TO KNOW Him! The feelings that were growing on the inside of me at that moment continue to grow even now. God's response continues to amaze me, and I truly believe that I hear Him because I take the time every day to spend quality time with Him.

How are you taking time each day to get to know God better and to develop an intimate relationship with Him? Does the thought of spending quality time with Him seem to interrupt your day or are you willing to make sacrifices? You may already have a well laid-out designated daily plan to ensure that you do what is absolutely necessary to be in God's presence.

Think about it. When we meet someone new, whether for business or personal, we have to invest time in getting to know the person. We are not haphazard in our dealings, and we take time to hold necessary conversations on the phone and in person to gain insight on the person's character. No matter what a person says, this cannot be obtained simply by text messages. We must have open dialogue.

That is exactly what prayer is– open dialogue with God. Several months ago, I was having a difficult day, and initially I wanted to text someone to pray for me. However, I decided not to send the text, and I covered myself in prayer.

And we are confident that he hears us whenever we ask for anything that pleases him. And since we know he hears us when we make our requests, we also know that he will give us what we ask for. 1 John 5:14-15

I was confident that in praying for what I was dealing with, God would calm my spirit and bring peace to the atmosphere. And He did just that. We don't have to be in a bowed down posture to pray. Sitting right at my desk, I prayed to God for what I needed and allowed Him to do what only He could do for me.

You must pray from your heart and remember to "never stop praying" (1 Thessalonians 5:17). Praying from the heart simply involves being open and honest with God about the most intimate desires from our heart. It doesn't have a list, specific agenda, or order in which the prayer is prayed. There isn't a teacher standing by to correct your pronunciation or to tell you to speak up and stand up straight or to tell you to stop crying and maintain eye contact. With open arms, God receives your prayers. Making Him a priority is the first and most important step in developing a plan to have a more intimate relationship with God.

If you don't make God a priority, you will allow busy schedules, the lack of desire to get up early in the morning, lack of time management, social media and other outside distractors to prevent you from keeping a commitment to spend time with God. When you place yourself, other people and things before

Chapter 1 | Spending Quality Time with God

God, you are making a conscious decision that these are more important than your Creator.

Identify a time that works best for you. Initially, an evening devotion time was best for me, but as I've mentioned before, my schedule changed, and I kept hearing God say, "Seek Me early." I knew that adjustments needed to be made. Early morning prayer may not be best for you due to other reasons. I encourage you to select the best time that works for you and stick to that time. It's interesting how people want God to stick to a timeline or hurry up with His intended plans, but they are flaky on keeping their commitments to Him, including a designated devotion and prayer time.

A rustling, loud, busy environment is not the best atmosphere for spending time with God. There are too many distractions. Find a quiet, uninterrupted space and time that can be devoted for you and God alone.

Develop an action plan for spending quality time with God.

1. Identify a specific time of day that you can dedicate to spend quality time with God.

2. Find a location where you won't be interrupted.

3. Determine a Bible reading plan and read your Bible daily while meditating on the scriptures. Pray and ask God to 'open up' the scriptures to you as you read. Ask for discernment.

4. Use a prayer journal to write down your prayers.

5. Identify a foundation scripture that you want to focus on during prayer.

6. Seek to hear what God wants to say to you.

7. Pray to God without being concerned with how you sound.

8. Write down a prayer list for yourself and for others.

Spending time with God will change your life.
Let me share an analogy with you. I went on a 25-mile Bike-the-Coast ride and during the ride, my right knee started to burn. And I mean really burn. One of the ladies from the Phoenix group, whom we had officially titled as our coach, rode up beside me and asked, "Which knee is hurting?"

After informing her that it was my right knee, she replied "Ok, now focus on the left."

I continued to pedal on while focusing on the left knee. By shifting my focus to the left knee, it took attention away from the burning I was feeling in my right knee. The direction of my thinking changed which allowed me to continue, refocus and enjoy the rest of the ride.

At the same time, I started praying again and thanking God for the opportunity and asking for the ability to finish the ride. Tears began to roll down my face, and I was hoping no one noticed. It wasn't because I was embarrassed. I just didn't want them to think it was from the burning in my knee. The tears were because of the confirmation that God would see me to the finish line, and He

Chapter 1 | Spending Quality Time with God

would not let me be harmed. I believe this happened because I spent quality time with Him. He continues to whisper affirmations of love into my mind and heart.

God is a loving God, and He wants to spend time with you. However, He is not going to force Himself on you or into your life. It is up to you to accept Him, learn of Him, trust Him, obey Him, and enjoy the journey of life with Him. Don't just look to God when things aren't going the way you think they should or when you need something. Don't blame God for the things that are happening in your life. Many times it is a person's actions that places him or her in certain situations. When things start to spiral out of control, they want to blame God. Everyone has free will; you will receive the blessings or the punishment for your choices.

I remember a time when I kept seeking God for an answer to a prayer, and I couldn't figure out why He *seemed* so silent. I knew He was with me, and my faith didn't falter. He was simply silent. One day I was listening to praise and worship music and a song that I'd heard before was playing. I thought about the prayer and the fact that I was receiving no answer from God. The song is Silence by Anthony Evans and while listening to the song I began to worship. I felt God's presence, and an overwhelming sense of peace came over me regarding the prayer. I released it and let it go because I trusted God, and I knew that He would always be with me.

Spending quality time with God will help you to understand that God is never late with answering a prayer. "The Father alone has the authority to set those dates and times, and they are not for you to know." (Acts 1:7 ERV) Isn't it interesting that when you want God to move and He doesn't move as fast as you want you have a tendency to get antsy and impatient? You want God to hurry up and move quickly to answer your prayers and reveal what you want to know. Flip the script. God tells you to do something, and you begin to question if you have the ability to do what He said. You delay in making a move, and all of a sudden you become silent to what He said. How is it that you want God to move quickly and yet, you're sometimes very slow at following His will and instructions for your life?

When you spend quality time with God, you won't be rushed or become frustrated when you need to make a decision. When everything on your job seems to be going against you, you won't be flustered because you spent time with God. I can attest to this as I was going through something at work and started interviewing for another job. I kept hearing God say, "Be still, and know that I am God!" (Psalm 46:10). I remained still and saw His glory revealed in my workplace. Had I not been spending quality time with Him, I would have missed the opportunity to see the salvation of the Lord.

Spending quality time with God is vital to your everyday growth. If you want to see the hand of God move in your life, you have to seek Him first and live a moral, upright life. You need to spend valuable quality time with God to grow in who you are in Him. Don't ever neglect the power of prayer and the strength you will gain as you pray to God every day and listen to His voice.

Seek the Kingdom of God above all else, and live righteously, and he will give you everything you need.

(Matthew 6:33)

Chapter 1 | Spending Quality Time with God

Love Yourself to Life

Chapter 2
Self-Talk

Fix your thoughts on what is true, and honorable, and right, and pure, and lovely, and admirable. Think about things that are excellent and worthy of praise.

Philippians 4:8

Let's talk about the "b" word. Now I know what you may be thinking. "Is she really going to talk about the "b" word? What is she trying to do? This is supposed to be an edifying book. Surely she is not really going to discuss the "b" word." Wait. Before you put the book down and give it a bad review, it's not that "b" word.

Why is it ok for some people to be ok with calling others the not-so-nice "b" word? It's even more unfortunate that for some, using this word is considered a "term of endearment" or an acceptable way to address friends. Well, not in my circle. We wouldn't dare call anyone the "b" word unless it is:

- Beautiful

- Beloved

- Blessing

- Boundless
- Brave
- Brilliant
- Balanced

See your friend as one who has:

- Big Vision
- Blisscipline (yes, that's a word)

Think about it. If you were applying for an employment position, would you put the not-so-nice "b" word on the application as a description for yourself? I would hope not. So why would it be acceptable to be addressed as so?

If you are one who uses the not-so-nice "b" word, I challenge you to begin addressing yourself and others by one of the positive words previously listed or another positive word that you would prefer. Even those of you who are not using that "b" word, try this on your friends. Be attentive to their reaction when you say…

"What's up beloved?"

"How are you doing blessing?"

"What have you been up to big vision?"

Chapter 2 | Self-Talk

You may be lifting the spirit of someone who is only accustomed to negative and derogatory self-talk. On the other hand, it may be you who needs to hear these words of affirmation. Make a list of eight positive words to say about yourself each day.

1. _____
2. _____
3. _____
4. _____
5. _____
6. _____
7. _____
8. _____

Whenever a negative descriptive word enters your mind, refute it with positive descriptive words. One negative thought may come, but replace it with multiple positive thoughts. Never let a negative thought have seed and take root and grow. Negative thoughts can interrupt your day and suck up your time. Negative thoughts can cause you to become distracted from what you're supposed to be doing.

There is a difference in the thought that you're never going to be anything versus God reminding you to do the things that He placed in your heart. The latter option does serve a purpose. It serves the purpose of reminding you that God gave you a specific vision, purpose, and job to do, but you aren't making any progress in following His desires for your life. You are following your own desires by not doing anything. You may have given up because you feel inadequate, and you care too much about what others think. Maybe you don't have a social media following, and you feel like you're not important. And maybe you have consistent thoughts of failure. You may even find yourself procrastinating. Whatever the reason, all of it embodies negative self-talk that keeps you from doing the things that you are created to do.

The negative self-talk is not real. Why entertain anything that has no foundation in who you are and what you can become? Think about it. Most of the time when you are entertaining negative self-talk, you've developed a full story with an unrealistic conclusion based on unrealistic characters, unrealistic conversations, and unrealistic emotions. Identify the stories that you are writing in your mind that aren't true. Stories that aren't relevant. Stories that aren't necessary. Stories that aren't helping you improve how you see yourself. More importantly, these are stories that do not align with who God says you are. With some of the stories and characters that you've imagined in your thoughts, maybe you should be writing a book. I'm just saying. Negative self-talk does not serve any purpose in helping you to be the person you are destined to be.

Bullying Thoughts

Negative self-talk can also be seen as bullying thoughts. Bullying thoughts are those thoughts that consistently attack your mind by 'saying' that you aren't good enough, pretty enough or successful enough. Those thoughts will tell you that love will never find you and that you will never get married and have children. They will tell you that you are a complete failure and that you are disgusting and stupid. They will have you thinking that you are either too fat or too skinny. Some of these statements may seem harsh, but they are real bullying thoughts that people experience. If any of these thoughts badger your mind, take control of the infestation of these bullying thoughts. If you think about it, your negative self-talk comes from something that happened in your past or something someone has said about you. I encourage you to not allow the past to bleed into your present and pollute your future.

Self-talk is the best talk when it is done appropriately. In addition to changing a negative thought to a positive thought you can:

- Go for a walk and enjoy nature and the many sounds that are in the air.

- Listen to a podcast, YouTube video, or upbeat music.

- Daydream Prayer for something you desire in your life.

- Enjoy a warm cup of tea with a relaxing posture.

- People watch and as a friend of mine said "make-up fun stories."
- Question the thought that interrupted your peace. Why is it there? Where did it originate from? What purpose is it serving?

When you change your thoughts, you change your life. Now it's time to do the work. Write 8 positive affirmations that you can say every morning and throughout the day. Start each declaration with I Am because each statement after the words I Am give further affirmation of who you are and who you desire to be.

1. _____
2. _____
3. _____
4. _____
5. _____
6. _____
7. _____
8. _____

Chapter 2 | Self-Talk

Tell yourself consistently how good you are. Talk yourself 'positive'! Some people wait on others to give them a "hoorah". Give yourself the best HOORAH you can. Encourage yourself, and be your own best cheerleader. Talk yourself into who you want to be. As you think, so are you.

Guard your heart above all else, for it determines the course of your life.
(Proverbs 4:23)

How you think about yourself sometimes calls for a CARE-Frontation. Not a CONfrontation but a CARE-Frontation. This CARE-Frontation may require you to identify the root of the negative thought and the negative self-impression you've formulated. This CARE-Frontation will require you to look at things that you criticize yourself for that other people could care less about. We've all had moments of self-criticizing only to find out that nobody noticed what we were concerned about. We have caused ourselves unnecessary self-inflicted mental drama.

This is where the CARE-Frontation comes in with the importance for you to identify the mental drama that you play out in your mind on a daily basis. This may cause you to have various emotions depending on who and what caused you to see yourself in a not-so-good light. Not addressing it causes something that is not real to appear real in your life.

Positive self-talk infuses you with the mentality you need to not give up or think that you cannot reach a goal. Don't be wishy-washy with your thoughts. Stand firm in what you believe to be true. Focus on your "I Am" declaration.

Keep vigilant watch over your heart; that's where life starts.
Don't talk out of both sides of your mouth; avoid careless banter, white lies,
and gossip. Keep your eyes straight ahead; ignore all sideshow distractions.
Watch your step, and the road will stretch out smooth before you.
Look neither right nor left; leave evil in the dust.

Proverbs 4:23-27 MSG

In 2016 and 2017, I hosted the Always Wear Your Tiara event. The purpose of the event is to encourage women to embrace the essence of who they are and not allow the past to interfere with their present and future. As I was praying and preparing for the first event, the idea came to me to have the women bring a 2x3 picture of themselves. Once they arrived, their picture was placed in a picture frame. After the women finished eating, I had them bring their picture to the table, and each woman had to speak positive encouraging words to their picture. Although this may sound strange to some people, it was and continues to be a powerful practice for some of the women. To change the process of what you say to yourself and how you say it takes practical action. Your self-talk will change your inner feelings and mindset and open you up to motivating yourself to step out of your comfort zone so that you can do great things.

The following quotes were written by some of the women who attended as they reflected on having to speak to their picture at the event.

Chapter 2 | Self-Talk

"I watched women close their eyes, fidget in their seats, take deep breaths, and gather their thoughts before they spoke– exposing their true discomfort before revealing the true essence of the matter. One by one they shared, and tears flowed. Strangely enough, looking into your own eyes through a picture brings an enlightenment beyond looking into a mirror. The person in that picture has existed before in a time and space that you can remember. The picture does not speak or move; the picture intently stares as if it's only listening.

I watched as women gave direct stares into the deepest parts of themselves. I watched as they revealed the secret parts of their thoughts, unmasking their disappointments, failures and shame. I listened to their insecurities but also hidden dreams of their futures.

My moment came and as I stared into my own eyes, I simply smiled and I started with three words: "I AM ENOUGH." In all my glorious imperfections, I am enough. It has taken moments of victory, defeat and paths of uncertainty to realize that I am sufficient for the task before me called "my life." I am well equipped even when I don't know it all. I'm settled in that. So in that moment I looked myself right in the eyes and gave myself a reminder that I AM ENOUGH. I am assured that with all that I don't possess, God will give me the rest along the way. I was built for my life, and so are YOU.

YOU ARE ENOUGH. God knew exactly where you would be in this moment and time in your life. Understand and know that it's all God needs to fulfill your purpose."

~Malissa Davis

"Having the privilege to facilitate one of the Always Wear Your Tiara sessions was so refreshing. Many times as women we spend much of our lives affirming others, giving to others and attempting to be all things to all people. We feel that if we do something for ourselves we are being selfish. If we say positive things about ourselves, we feel as though we are steeped in pride. The latter is especially true if we are parents. We will make sure our children have everything they need and oftentimes what they want. This is noble, but in the process we neglect one of the most important people in the equation – ourselves. We will lavish others with words of affirmation in telling them how beautiful, intelligent, courageous, and phenomenal they are, yet we rarely, if ever, take the time to speak those kind words of affirmation to ourselves. It can be perceived as narcissistic to tell yourself how awesome, smart, brave and beautiful you are.

At the Always Wear Your Tiara event, each of the ladies was asked to bring a picture of themselves, and when we arrived we were given a beautiful frame to put the picture in. We were also given a Tiara to wear throughout the event. We were each asked to look at our picture and speak to the woman we saw in the picture. In other words, we were encouraged to exercise some positive self-talk. Some women spoke to the little girl they used to be, and they reminded her that she was not responsible for what happened to her whether it was abuse, rejection, or abandonment. Some spoke forgiveness for past failures and mistakes. Others boldly proclaimed that they were enough. Lots of tears were shed, and it was perfectly okay because Monica DeBro created a safe environment for women to be vulnerable so that we could have the opportunity

Chapter 2 | Self-Talk

to flush out all the toxic strongholds that held us captive way too long. In those precious moments we were being reminded of our value and worth. We embraced the fact that loving ourselves, no matter what, was the strength we needed to rise to the occasion to be and do all that God has purposed for our lives.

~Minister Evelyn Gaskin

"The 2016 Always Wear Your Tiara event was a surprisingly unexpected time of sharing, discovery, transparency and deliverance. As I am looking at my portrait and writing this paragraph, tears are flowing. When the women were speaking to their portrait, I clearly remember feeling overwhelmed and overtaken with fear, uneasiness and vulnerability. Most of all I was saying to myself, 'I really do not want to do this. Not right now, and definitely not in front of these amazing ladies.' However, as everyone shared and tears flowed, I too had to share. As I looked at my picture and began to speak, I spoke words in relation to what other people said to me. In that moment, I said things to myself that was very different from what I actually believed. It was not easy and definitely uncomfortable. I can't remember all the specific words I verbalized as I looked at my picture but as I spoke, a heavy and loaded weight was lifted. I sensed the power of the following words: 'I am beautiful inside and out. I am worthy of love and to be loved. I am worthy of shining while not feeling guilty or feeling the need to dim my light so others can shine brighter.' Since the event I still have moments in which I need to remind myself of who God says I am. Nevertheless, I am forever grateful for such a spiritually eye-opening experience and opportunity. Every time I look at my picture, I fondly remember the event and see a renewed me. My picture captures and solidifies 2 Corinthians 5:17: 'This means that anyone who belongs to Christ has become a new person. The old life is gone; a new life has begun!' My picture represents my present and future filled with love, hope, goodness, faith, growth, promise, overcoming and winning."

~**Marie-Eve Thomas**

"It is easy to put myself down either through thinking I am not as qualified as the next person or by telling myself I was stupid for thinking that something big could happen to or for me or even thinking it was something I did wrong when I find myself hitting the brick wall. When I was told that we would be speaking to ourselves, I thought, 'Okay. No biggie.' Little did I realize that it would be very emotional to speak positive things to myself. As I looked at one of many selfies that I took, tears began to flow. My throat tightened and my voice cracked as I began to tell myself that I was enough. Initially as the words left my mouth, I didn't feel empowered; I felt like running. But through this process I realized that running was what I was good at, and I needed to sit, hear and know that I was enough.

I was enough for what God has purposed for me.

No one else is enough for my purpose at this moment in time."

~**Cherry Davis-Cook**

"Speaking to myself that day was life changing! It really opened up my eyes to see how negative I was towards myself, but I also realized how positive I was towards others. It was very emotional because it allowed me to really look at myself in a different light and tell myself that despite all the hurt,

Chapter 2 | Self-Talk

struggles and rough patches of life, I was still standing and smiling! I am now more mindful of negative self-talk, and I remind myself of how far I have come. It was also so comforting to know that so many other women who are phenomenal in my eyes also struggle with viewing themselves positively so hearing their self-talk was also very encouraging. I am very grateful for Monica who continues to encourage, empower and support women in helping us to see ourselves as Queens. She helps us to love ourselves to life, and she reminds us to always speak positively about ourselves."

~Melinda DeLeon

"As I sat there intentionally focused on that picture of myself, I was flooded with emotions. I could truly see the woman before me, someone I had forgotten about at times. I began to speak to the life I saw. I was overwhelmed with the love of God and the support of my sisters as they intently listened to me. To hear the words of strength, encouragement, and truth come out of me 'to me' reignited a passion inside of me. It was the passion of a love that says I am more than enough and that I am worth dying for.
It was a passion of a love that says I am lovable and worthy of love and that I have been given much, and I can freely give."

~ Estella Smith

"The Always Wear Your Tiara event was an event that created an impact in my life. I went to meet a few wonderful women. I went with an open mind not knowing what to expect. I felt so much joy when Monica mentioned that all the women there were called by name and that we were there called for His purpose.

49

I certainly went in with an expectation of speaking to a few Christian women, but little did I expect that the woman I would be speaking to would be me. It is easy to talk to women to encourage them and to be there for them as a friend. It's easy to try to help heal the broken hearted, but healing and talking to yourself is not an easy task.

Talking to myself with my picture in front of me helped me realize that I always looked outside for help to heal and that I was always trying to help someone else. It also made me realize that my greatest strength comes from within me. I realized that I needed healing. I needed someone to talk to. I figured out that I was my own best friend.

In a way, it set me free to be heard and to be understood. I had so much to talk about. I had so much to say to myself. I had forgotten to tell myself these things in the busyness of life.

It also helped me realize that a woman's heart is strong. She can endure a lot more than she can imagine. Listening to other women made me realize how much others go through. It was also very comforting how the women in the group encouraged each other.

I am thankful to Monica for introducing me the concept of talking to myself. It can be called self-healing. I had a great time at the Always Wear Your Tiara event, and I hope that other women also have the same experience that I did."

~Venetia Michael

"Speaking to my picture during the Always Wear Your Tiara event was

Chapter 2 | Self-Talk

refreshing and a reminder of who I am. God, who is the GREAT I AM, gifted me to become the person that I am today. I had previously allowed negative seed to be planted in my mind. So speaking to myself was empowering and encouraging, and it let me know what I really thought about myself. It reminded me that I am fearfully and wonderfully made by a great creator."

~Cheree McArn

"Have you ever stood and thought to yourself that all the odds were against you or that you couldn't do something, or that you weren't good enough? When I had the honor of being invited to an Always Wear Your Tiara event, I had no Idea how much of an impact it would have on my life. The topic of speaking positive to myself really hit home. It was more than just speaking positive which is something I always tried to do. It was really about making positive affirmations to and about myself, and it gave me a clear vision and a clear sight of God's purpose for my life. For me, it was a daily process of saying what I believed myself to be. I was always quick to tell someone else that they were beautiful, but I never spoke those affirmations to myself. Every morning when I sit up in my bed I have my framed picture of myself that I got from the event, and I look at that beautiful person staring back at me. I tell her something positive. I tell her that she is beautiful and that she is successful and that she is brave."

~Danielle Esdale

Here is something to consider regarding self-talk: If God doesn't call you by certain names, why should you? If God doesn't call you by negative names, why should you allow others to call you by those names?

God doesn't say, "Come here stupid."

"What are you up to ugly?"

"You can't find anything to do loser?"

Of course He doesn't call you by those names. Instead, He boldly declares that "Wisdom is yours, all you have to do is ask." (James 1:5-6) "Go where I am leading you beautiful one." (Psalm 32:8) "You are a success because I have plans for you!" (Jeremiah 29:11)

As you can see, the words sometimes spoken or taking up room in your mind during self-talk need to reflect how God sees you and what He has to say about you. It will be difficult to tap into what God has for you in the future if you remain in a place where the negative self-talk begins or if you don't address negative self-talk that interrupts your thoughts.

Consider this—does anyone invite negative self-talk to come into their mind? I don't think anyone is sitting around saying, "Bring on the negativity." You shouldn't entertain the accusatory seeds through words that Satan plants in your mind. As soon as you recognize it, do SOMETHING to immediately change those thoughts. You can't stop conversations from forming in your head, but you can identify them in order to control and challenge them. Identify the source and know that God will never call you anything that doesn't align with His word. Once you identify the thought, it will open the ability to change the negative into a positive. The longer it takes for you to address the negative thought, the more negative emotions are building up on the inside of you. Take captive of every thought so that it doesn't take captive of you! Here's an idea– even when you are having a good thought, make it a better thought.

Only you can change the reflection of your self-talk. Others can encourage and motivate you, but you have to believe in yourself. Now is the time to daily confess and BELIEVE in the goodness within you.

Chapter 3
Your Surroundings

For God is not a God of disorder but of peace.
(1 Corinthians 14:33a)

It is very important that you are attentive to your surroundings. This is something that you have to always be aware of because negativity can creep in without you inviting it into your thoughts and environment. First Corinthians 14:33 in the English Standard Version Bible reads, "For God is not a God of confusion but of peace." If your surroundings are disheveled and out of order, it won't result in a peaceful environment. If your thoughts are negative and causing confusion in your mind, it won't bring you peace. God is a God of peace!

What if it's not your thoughts that are disrupting the peace in your environment? There are some people who are known to have a negative spirit. They are always complaining about one thing or another. They believe that everything that happens is always someone else's fault. Day after day, month after month, year after year, they are saying the same things and complaining about the same things. For me, if I provide guidance or options on making the necessary adjustments and they still continue to go in the same circle, I stop discussing it and avoid the conversation all together.

Insanity has been defined as doing the same thing over and over and expecting different results. ~Merriam Webster Dictionary

I won't be on the insanity Ferris wheel with anyone. Entertaining negativity will eventually rub off onto you if you are not careful. I surround myself with positive people. With this in mind, I am not saying that we don't have sporadic days where things are not going the way we expected. However, we discuss the issue, develop a plan, and start taking the necessary steps to see the plan evolve into its projected intention.

There will be times when you have to pull back from relationships with people because of their negativity and draining spirit. Have you ever known someone who absolutely drained your emotions and spirit whenever they came around? What adjustments did you make? Sometimes an honest and open conversation with the person will help. He or she may not know that they are exuding a characteristic that is not supportive of the relationship, whether it is personal, business, or casual. Lack of awareness allows people to continue with their current behavior. Other times, you may need to pull back from the relationship and allow yourself some time to be able to identify how to make the relationship healthier.

I've had someone call me on the phone and tell me that they were going to write me off and not have any further dealings with me. Initially, the statement

Chapter 3 | Your Surroundings

hit me with a sense of unbelief; I was wondering what I had done. The person continued the conversation by saying that they were corrected by their counselor because they were making an inaccurate judgement and assessment. I had not done anything to cause angst in the relationship, but because of the way the person felt about someone who was close to me, they projected those feelings towards me as well.

This conversation caused discomfort and disappointment because I often wondered what would happen if I needed to have a "tough love" conversation with the person. How would it be received? Would the person be easily offended? Would the tough love conversation be received? Would self-reflection occur? If it is so easy for someone to be ready to write me off, it places a strain on the relationship and decreases the level of trust. It decreases the trust factor so much that it would cause me to pause and think about walking on eggshells in order to keep the person from being easily offended. Notice I said 'think about' because I can guarantee you that it would only be a thought. When you walk on eggshells around people, it doesn't allow you to be your true self. It places too many walls and barriers in the environment. It isn't a secure setting and at any moment the volcano of emotions will erupt causing even more division in the relationship. If you find yourself in a relationship with someone that you have to walk on eggshells around, whether it be a personal or professional relationship, it is not a healthy one.

You can cause your own pain when you are not attentive to how you're responding to others and by allowing others to treat you with disregard and disrespect. This involves in person communication, text messages, email, and social media. If you know that different aspects or people on social media disturb your thinking, avoid interacting or entertaining what doesn't bring you peace and satisfaction. Simply unfollow the person or persons.

A close friend of mine and I were talking one day, and she mentioned Bike the Coast. This is a bike ride along the coast of Oceanside, CA, and the options were for a 25, 50, or 100 mile ride. Being the person I am, I invited myself along for the adventure. During this time, I was trying new things and venturing outside of my comfort zone. Participating in a 25 mile bike ride was definitely outside of anything that I ever thought I would do. It didn't help that I knew I was going to be participating in this ride with people who had the higher level bikes. I had a one gear cruiser bike. At one point I thought about purchasing another bike with gears to help me be successful, but my friend assured me that I would be ok on the cruiser bike.

In reflection, if I had gotten a bike with multiple gears, I would have been like David when Saul applied his warrior gear on David to fight Goliath. Sure, I would have had time to practice riding the bike with gears, but that still would not have prepared me for the ride. I would have been riding the bike and not really knowing the purpose of the gears or how or when to adjust the gears for the hills along the ride. I know this because as my friend was riding up one of the hills, one of the bikers told her in passing that she needed to adjust the gears.

Chapter 3 | Your Surroundings

Therefore, purchasing a new bike to participate in the ride was not going to adequately prepare me. I have had bikes with gears in the past and didn't know what to do with them and for this ride, it would've been the same. Plus, all I wanted to do was hang out with my friend and participate in something fun, new, and adventurous.

So I ask, what is it that you enjoy spending time doing? Are you making a conscious effort to do those things or making excuses? Think about all of the things that you make excuses for...not starting a business, not seeking opportunities to travel and see more than your immediate surroundings, not starting a relationship because you don't have confidence in who you are or you don't believe that you could meet a certain person's standards. I've talked with numerous people who continue to make excuses for not going back to school for a degree they have always wanted. Excuses include mostly money and the time commitment. My response is that time is going to pass whether you are making the most of it or not. Time does not stand still. Nor can you go back and remove or change events from the past. Time will keep going, and you have to do what it does– keep moving forward.

Sometimes your surroundings are in the confines of your mind. Your attitude can get you in a world of trouble in your current surroundings. Are you the type of person who always has the response that you are who you are and that you won't change your attitude for anybody? If so then how can you expect God to do a new thing in you when you have an old attitude?

"And no one puts new wine into old wineskins. For the wine would burst the wineskins, and the wine and the skins would both be lost. New wine calls for new wineskins."

(Mark 2:22)

You cannot expect new progress with the same attitude, the same negativity, and the same mental images and thoughts that suggest that it is everyone else's fault but yours. New beginnings require a new mindset just as it is not good to put new wine in old wineskins. To grow, you need a new mindset for change. Be attentive to the thoughts in your mental surroundings.

Most days when I am home during the day, I have music playing to help keep me focused. I have realized that the television is a distraction when I am trying to accomplish something. One day, the carpet cleaners arrived at my home, and the music was playing as usual. When they were done cleaning the carpet, one of them asked, "What kind of music is that?"

I answered, "Praise and worship."

To my surprise, the young man said, "That's jolly music. I like it."

I've never thought of praise and worship music as jolly music, but I guess it is.

There are other times when I will play sermons or motivational speeches from a CD or YouTube. I like this aspect many times because it is instilling more of God's Word in me, and that allows me to continue to see myself and grow as an individual. The subject of the sermons or messages I listen to depend on

Chapter 3 | Your Surroundings

what my goals and/or challenges are at that moment.

When you find yourself having a negative countenance, be attentive to what you are watching on television. I mentioned this in my first book, and I feel that it is worth mentioning again here. What you watch on television can influence your personality and emotions. Don't believe me? Take a break from watching certain shows on television and stop listening to music that is not uplifting. You will see how much you can grow and how your reactions to others will change. Here's my example of this. I was watching Say Yes to the Dress on a regular basis. It was interesting seeing the women try on different dresses and hearing the responses of their families and friends. At one point my attitude started to change while watching. I started to cry and feel sad. After this continued to happen time and time again, I realized that I was becoming emotional as a result of my singleness. This isn't a television show with women demeaning each other or cursing each other out. It is simply women seeking to find their dream wedding dress to say yes to. However, it still caused a negative reaction in which I had to pull back and take time to regain my senses. At some point, I was able to start watching it again. I recognized that my environment and emotions were being affected so I took necessary actions to make adjustments. I challenge you to see how television and music are playing a part in your everyday emotions and reactions to others.

Know your surroundings! Now it's time to do the work to ensure that you are in a healthy environment that supports your ability to **Love Yourself to Life!**

Love Yourself to Life

Identify 4 things in your surroundings that cause a negative response. Then write down some adjustments that you will **intentionally take** for a resolution.

1. _____
2. _____
3. _____
4. _____

Identify 4 positive things in your surroundings that allow you to **Love Yourself to Life!** These are things that you will keep around.

5. _____
6. _____
7. _____
8. _____

Chapter 3 | Your Surroundings

Love Yourself to Life

Chapter 4
Avoid the Comparison Trap

Pay careful attention to your own work, for then you will get the satisfaction of a job well done, and you won't need to compare yourself to anyone else. For we are each responsible for our own conduct.

(Galatians 6:4-5)

Comparing yourself to someone else is a trap, and it can take away your joy. You will either become inflated with your own ego or deflated at the thought of not being good enough. The comparison trap can make you feel uncomfortable in your own environment. What works for one person is not guaranteed to work for you.

Consider how it makes you feel when you start comparing yourself to the success of someone else. This comparison can be based on the other person's professional success, relationship developing, engagement, marriage, pregnancy, new family, business growth, home, car, travel, promotion, and the list goes on and on. There are times when people even compare their ability to pray to how other people pray. As mentioned in another section of the book, spending time with God will increase your openness and comfort with prayer.

What feelings erupt when the comparison mode starts in your mind? Do you find comfort in comparing yourself to others?

We've all at one point or another compared ourselves to others. But once we learn better, we do better. We learn that what is for one person is not for us. When we find ourselves comparing, God will send someone at the right time to defuse what we've built up in our minds.

For example, there was a moment in which I was comparing an event that I have been hosting for a couple of years to someone else's event. The Elephant in the Room is an event in which we discuss topics that are often avoided but absolutely necessary to discuss. Some of the topics have included domestic violence, depression, suicide, finances, and physical health. I found myself looking at how the other event was organized. I was looking at their influential speakers, sponsors, support from the online community, etc. I was looking at the spiritual aspect of the event, and I started to pull back from beginning the preparation stage for the next Elephant in the Room event.

Little did I know, the very person who was hosting and leading that event would be the one I would be holding a conversation with the very same week. I am a very open and transparent person, and I shared with her what I was thinking and feeling. Immediately, she dispelled every negative thought that was rolling around in my mind, and she boldly informed me that I was not cancelling The Elephant in the Room. She said that it was a much needed event and that people should attend to receive the information. Needless to say, God didn't allow me to remain in that void area of comparing.

Chapter 4 | Avoid the Comparison Trap

When I was in Arkansas for my sister Laura's 60th birthday, I spent some time with a dear friend of mine. She began to share with me about a past relationship. Although she was going through a turbulent time in her life, someone "looking in" through a stained glass window envied what she saw. My friend made a statement that has stuck with me; "people envy what they don't know." I have never forgotten the statement and asked her to share her experience of someone falling into the comparison trap.

"Years ago when I was married, I met a lady at church. Over the years our families became good friends. She and I talked daily. Our children played together, and we worshipped God together. She was my friend! We remained friends over the years, but then her calls decreased. I would always be the one making the call. Our conversations became almost nonexistent, but I still considered her my friend. Then one day she upped and moved away without saying a word. It really hurt me because I thought we were better friends. And I didn't know where she was.

Many, many years passed us by, but eventually via internet I was able to find her. So I asked her why she left the state without a mere goodbye, and she told me these three words. She said, "I envied you!" You and your husband always seemed happy. Ya'll laughed and had so much fun, and I wanted what ya'll had. You always seemed to have it together, and you were always so strong.

But little did she know, I was unhappy within that relationship that she "envied". See she envied what she didn't know.

Fast forward to present time, I've been divorced for almost 18 years. She's still married to the same man!"

~Wanda Artis

Seeing someone else's life through a stain glass window will make things appear as something beautiful. You will be under the delusion that all is well and that they live a life filled with vibrant colors and that nothing negative ever happens to them. Seeing through a stained glass window will give you a false-reality and never allow you to know what is happening on the other side of what appears to be a beautiful window. In reality, it's shattered glass with layers of colored tape to hold it together. While you see beauty, the woman on the other side of the glass sees brokenness, struggle, pain, and captivity. Maybe she's being held captive to her own thoughts and negative beliefs about herself. Maybe she's being held captive due to fear and unforgiveness. At other times, she may be held captive in an abusive relationship because at the time she doesn't see a way out.

Many times people don't know what is happening behind closed doors. They don't see the abuse occurring within the relationship. As a result, people will envy someone not really knowing what they are dealing with on a daily basis. They may start to pull away because of what they think they know and want for themselves. They may allow what appears to be good from what they see on the outside contaminate how they feel about themselves on the inside through envy. Every time you find yourself in the comparison trap, Satan is stealing your joy. Be very careful when you look through what appears to be a

Chapter 4 | Avoid the Comparison Trap

beautiful stain glass window!

You see, we see relationships building and forming not knowing if one of them is settling because he or she has a fear of remaining single. The person they have settled to be with does not meet specific non-negotiable qualities they want in a mate. However, because they are comparing their singleness to their friends who are "booed up", they choose to settle. Eventually, the one who settled will realize that they should've waited on the one with the non-negotiable qualities.

People have a tendency to wear masks and only allow others into their lives only to a certain point in order to keep them from knowing their reality. They have a reality filled with scars: spiritual, emotional, physical, mental, and financial scars. Oh how the mask can be worn to imply that everything is going well, but if the mask was removed and transparency was allowed, one could see the hurting people sitting right next to them. The person sitting right next to you could appear like they have it all together, but in reality, they are in desperate need for help, true help.

Comparing and observing others are not the same. Observing others is beneficial as it can provide you with insight on how to improve in an area. For example, I observe other websites to see how to improve www.loveyourselftolife.co. I read blogs to see how I can become a better writer. When considering my writing style, I soon found out that I needed clarity because I realized that writing papers for school is very different from writing a blog. I also watch YouTube videos to learn how to become a more creative and engaging speaker. Taking the time to observe others allows you to be open to growth so that you won't remain stagnant in commonality.

When you come to really know who you are, you aren't easily moved by people or things. Be confident in who you are. Acknowledge your strengths and weaknesses as this will help you identify areas in which you need to take steps to improve your current strategies and skills. Instead of comparing yourself to someone else, identify who you are and how you can become better by leveraging your strengths. In order to attain happiness and satisfaction in the work you do, you definitely have to use your strengths and believe in and love whatever it is you are working for.

Understanding who you are will make you more confident and more comfortable with your current status. You won't be tempted to compare yourself to someone else who has a different passion than the one you have. Have a clear grasp of who you are and what you can do each day to be the person you want to be within the next 24 hours or the next week or the next month or the next year, and years to come. Why do I say within the next 24 hours? Sometimes we find ourselves struggling in an area. We are not meant to stay in **THAT** moment. And because of that, we have to do something to make immediate changes. The change may not be drastic but necessary in order to have some clarity about the struggle you are currently experiencing. You can make changes now for a better tomorrow.

We can compare ourselves to others for various reasons. As previously mentioned I was considering purchasing another bike for Bike the Coast.

Chapter 4 | Avoid the Comparison Trap

Comparing my bike to others almost made me spend money on a new bike that would have been unnecessary for me to spend. Plus, I would have been riding on one of those "little" seats. That would've been even more uncomfortable for me. Life will surround you with many people, and this will give you multiple opportunities to play the comparison game. You will compare yourself with the outer appearance, home, car, job, family, finances, gifts, talents, and abilities of others. And the list can go on and on. If you want to improve on the inside by avoiding the comparison trap as well as improve on the outside, show up, do the work, and go after your own goals.

When you show up, does the real 'you' show up or is it a counterfeit of someone else? Do you minimize your personality to fit in with others so that they are more comfortable? I have a big personality, and I can't imagine shrinking it down just to satisfy someone else. I don't want to find myself not enjoying life because I am more concerned about how others see me.

Eight Things to do to Avoid the Comparison Trap

1. Focus on who God says you are and what He says about you.

2. Know and truly believe that you are a fearfully and wonderfully made individual.

3. Don't allow social media to send you on a downward spiral in your mind. Remember that social media is a snapshot of what people want you to see. Social media has become the ultimate example of seeing someone's life through a stain glass window. You may need to delete

some people from your social media circle.

4. Take quiet moments to get to know you (reconnect with yourself) to eliminate the inner critic.

5. Write a daily declaration with positive affirmations to read throughout the day. Even if it is something that you do not see in yourself right now, declare it.

6. Here's a thought: Compare yourself to yourself. Take time to assess where you are right now. Think about the accomplishments that you've made. Compare that to where you want to be in the future. To do what others are doing, do your research, get the training, ask questions, and practice your skill. Become very gifted at your skill through practice and obtaining feedback. One of my goals is to become more active with speaking engagements. I have a plan in place to reach this goal. Be creative with the methods that you take to get to where you see yourself in the future.

7. Always keep in mind that you don't know the price the person had to pay in order to get what they have. Avoid the Stain Glass Window Syndrome.

8. Most importantly, to avoid the comparison trap, pray and ask God to engrave on your heart and mind how important you are to Him. At the name of Jesus, demons must flee. I am a believer that anything that doesn't align with God's Word is a demon. Those defeating

negative thoughts that come during the comparison episodic stories that you're playing in your mind are not from God. While praying, ask God to show you even more of who you are and what you can do to flourish in the area(s) He had commanded for you to occupy.

Don't change yourselves to be like the people of this world, but let God change you inside with a new way of thinking.

Then you will be able to understand and accept what God wants for you. You will be able to know what is good and pleasing to him and what is perfect.
(Romans 12:2 ERV)

Chapter 5
Invest in Yourself

If you want to invest in something with minimum risks and a guaranteed big return, invest in yourself.

~Unknown

In this chapter we are going to discuss the four letter word, GOAL. You may have a specific goal in mind that you want to reach within the next 24 hours or the next 6 months or the next year or the next several years even. Whatever your goal is, you have to take time to invest in yourself in order to reach the goal. Whether this investment is setting aside a specific time each week to work on your goal, identifying resources needed to reach your goal or knowing how much money it is going to take to reach your goal, you need to invest in yourself. I once read that if you don't have a goal, you are only existing. Well, I don't want you to only exist. I want you to excel at your dreams, desires, and goals.

Before you read any further, I want you to identify 8 areas in which you can invest in yourself.

1. _____
2. _____

3. _____

4. _____

5. _____

6. _____

7. _____

8. _____

Now that you've identified your eight areas, I will share with you eight ways in which I invest in myself.

1. Attend/Volunteer at weekly church services on Wednesday and Sunday

2. Healthy community of friends

3. Life Coach and a Health Coach

4. Inspirational and Motivational CDs and YouTube videos

5. Reading and listening to books

6. Simply taking time to relax

7. Online training courses

8. Attending various workshops, conferences, and seminars

Chapter 5 | Invest in Yourself

How do you visualize the end result of your GOAL? In writing this book, there were days that I didn't want to write, and it was hard to focus. I had to start treating the writing process as one that was required for school. There were specific deadlines to meet when I was in school which required me to have a razor-sharp focus or my grade would be reduced.

That razor-sharp focus included dedicating 5pm – 9pm every weekday (except Wednesday), Saturday morning and Sunday afternoon to research and writing. My doctoral project required my dedication and support from family and friends in order for me to be successful. The support from family and friends came in to play even more during the last 16 weeks of studies. I informed all of them either by text or posting on social media that from 5pm – 9pm, I would not be available to talk or text. They respected this blocked-out time to the point that if they called, they started the conversation with… "I know I only have 5 minutes before you go into lockdown, but I have a question or I just needed to talk to you about something."

During this time, I did not get on social media, watch television, talk on the phone, text, or do anything that distracted me from completing my GOAL. The last 16 weeks did not allow me to slow down and get off track. Any small deviation that would have prevented me from remaining on task would have caused a challenge for me in being able to meet the expectations set by my statistician, mentor, and course facilitator. The established schedule was non-negotiable. Now, I am aware that emergencies can happen, and I am thankful that I was saved from any unforeseen circumstances.

The point is I established a plan in order to reach a GOAL that I wanted to reach. I had to remain committed to the goal and adjust if an emergency did arise. I wasn't caught up on what was being posted on social media because I knew it would be a time stealer. It would literally steal precious time and energy that I needed to spend on something that was more beneficial.

While social media is great, it can definitely be a time stealer from your day. How many times have you logged-on to social media for a quick moment and then later realized that it's been at least an hour? Time flies especially on social media channels. During my lock-down time, if I wanted to get on social media, it would be after 9pm or later, if I needed to spend additional time writing.

Investing in yourself can be framed by three things:

1. Environment
2. Education
3. Experience

In considering these three attributes, how do they currently support you professionally and personally? In what ways can you make an investment in these areas to become better at what you're currently doing?

You can't do anything about yesterday, but you can definitely do something about today and your many tomorrows. How you invest in yourself today will determine your many tomorrows. Investing in yourself will help you become

Chapter 5 | Invest in Yourself

Prepared for your Position within your Purpose and grant you Privileges that you wouldn't ordinarily have. Investing in yourself will prevent you from shrinking in the presence of opportunity. Your success is dependent upon how you adapt to necessary changes and make adjustments.

Until you take hold of and embrace who you are meant to be, your legacy will never be fulfilled. You have a dream and a vision; now it's time to take action. It doesn't cost anything to write the vision and make it plain! Make some type of faith move so that God knows you're serious.

1. What is your dream?

2. How do you visualize that dream once it is fulfilled?

3. What action are you prepared to take to make the dream become a reality?

4. Identify 3 resources that you will need.

5. What online courses or classroom courses do you need to take to get prepared?

6. Who can be an effective mentor?

7. If you need to make financial adjustments, how can you start saving for the financial investment that will be needed?

8. Identify your team who will keep you accountable at different stages of your progress.

When you select a mentor or accountability team, it needs to be a person or persons who will not allow you to make excuses for not completing tasks. They need to be able to provide constructive input to help you remain focused, and you need to be ready to receive it. A real accountability partner will push you to hold firm to due dates and expectations. This person will intentionally not allow you to make excuses for why things aren't getting done. You will need to have an accountability partner that you respect and don't want to let down because you are doing what you're supposed to do. Making excuses will ultimately keep you behind schedule. Here are a few things to consider with investing in yourself and developing in certain areas:

1. Develop razor-sharp focus to identify, walk-in and live out your purpose.

2. Develop an attitude of a winner to stay focused on your vision.

3. Develop a deep level of honesty to embrace the need for assistance.

4. Develop thick skin to be able to handle constructive criticism.

5. Develop the ability to not allow naysayers to discourage you and keep you in the same position.

6. Develop the proficiency of connecting with people who will help expand your purpose.

7. Develop and keep developing your strengths while learning from your weaknesses.

Chapter 5 | Invest in Yourself

8. Develop, keep, and maintain an intimate relationship with God. Pray and ask Him for wisdom and an increase in discernment.

In everything, remember that quiet time is a wise investment for your future! Quiet time allows for reflection and the ability to receive accurate directions.

Chapter 6
Motivation and Purpose

"Don't allow people who are not a part of your purpose, interfere with your future."

~Dr. Monica DeBro

A lazy person is as bad as someone who destroys things.

Proverbs 18:9

If you are slow in your work, you are slow in fulfilling your purpose. When you want to learn and grow in your purpose, do you take the necessary steps? If so, what are they? If not, you are wasting time. What are you waiting on? Are you waiting until you have it all together to take a step towards your purpose? Do you think others had it all together when they took the leap of faith? The truth of the matter is that someone is waiting on you to step out in your purpose so that they can have a breakthrough. Someone is waiting on you to write your story so that they can know that they can survive despite what they are going through just as you did. God did not bless you with gifts, talents, abilities, and a purpose for you to not do anything with them.

In order to reach the purpose God has placed on your life, you need an organized plan. There is a guarantee that your plan will change and when it does, grow in the ability to be flexible. Be flexible, but stay FOCUSED. Don't allow an adjustment to derail you from making progress. Taking a leap without having a plan isn't a set-up for success. Plan out HOW you're going to meet your goal. Seek out the assistance of someone who has done what you are trying to do and gain insight from them. Remember you will need to invest in yourself to reach the goals you want to meet.

There isn't a benefit if you develop a plan and not do any work towards seeing the plan and vision fulfilled. It is worthless time spent when you brainstorm to come up with ideas for success and never do anything with the ideas. Not acting on it allows your dreams to die with you.

The graveyard is the richest place on the surface of the earth because there you will see the books that were not published, ideas that were not harnessed, songs that were not sung, and drama pieces that were never acted.
~Dr. Myles Munroe

Without realizing where you are and where you want to be, you'll remain in the same stagnant position. One thing for sure, I don't want to live and die without living up to my full potential. I want you to keep pushing yourself and live life out loud. Live life out loud beyond what others and even you expect. Live life out loud until you don't recognize yourself.

Chapter 6 | Motivation and Purpose

The first few months after finishing my doctoral studies, I felt lost and didn't know what to do. I failed to plan what the next steps would be once I finished school. Planning is not a new concept by no means. However, failing to plan resulted in me feeling as though I was walking in a wilderness season. It took me a few months to identify what was going on as I initially thought I was "ok". Then I realized that my norm had changed.

No longer did I have the same stringent school schedule that required me to write and submit discussion posts, papers, and PowerPoint presentations. My work-life-school balance had drastically changed. For two years I had kept the close-to same schedule, and that schedule was no longer necessary or relevant because the degree completion requirements had been met. No longer did I need to go to the coffee shop to write from the time I got off of work until the shop closed. My Saturday mornings and Sunday afternoon/evenings were free. While I was excited to have accomplished my goal, I felt lost. In speaking with others who had finished doctoral studies, they had similar experiences. Our norm as we once knew it had ended which resulted in a need to shift.

At some time in May, I made the decision to not focus on my purpose, but to enjoy the remainder of 2017 by meeting new people, trying new things, and traveling. I had to learn to relax and be ok with not being on the computer. In June, I text messaged a friend of mine to ask if she wanted to go on a cruise with me in July. She responded back by the time I finished teaching my class, and we were booked by 5pm on the same day. In my run of trying new things, I rented bicycles and rode through downtown Phoenix, went to two birthday parties of people I didn't know, went to watch the NBA finals with a group of people I didn't know, started going out to listen to live music with another group of people I didn't know, and participated in Bike the Coast for a 25 mile bike ride along the coast of Oceanside, CA.

Spending time in London and then taking a beautiful train ride to Paris during the week of Christmas was an unexpected adventure. I had talked about it for a few weeks and finally planned it out a week before Christmas. In planning this vacation, I was going back and forth with my decision. I thought about cancelling the trip because I was thinking that I could work and make extra money at the hospital instead. My friend Marie-Eve said, "When you are on your deathbed, you are not going to be saying, 'I wish I had worked those extra shifts at the hospital.'" At that point, the idea of cancelling no longer existed. I was going to experience London and Paris, and I am not disappointed with that choice.

The biggest of the new adventures was signing up for a Tour of Israel. This happened because I started attending a singles ministry group (another new adventure), and I read a flyer that was on the table. I began praying about whether this was something for me to do, and a few days later I watched a video on the website. I was overflowed with an emotion releasing me to join others on the Tour of Israel. As I processed in my mind what I was planning to do, I never thought I would be going to Israel. Nor did I think I would be going without my family and that it would be with a group of people that I didn't know. Typically, when it is a big trip such as the one to London, Paris

Chapter 6 | Motivation and Purpose

and Israel, it includes my sisters. This was going to be different.

I share my experiences about exploring because in my mind, I was on vacation from hosting events and speaking. I was focused on having fun and only hosting the already planned event for 2017– The Elephant in the Room June session.

In the midst of me enjoying "my time off", Minister Evelyn Gaskin walked by me at church one Sunday and God spoke to me and said, "That's your speaker for Always Wear Your Tiara." My response was, "Ok in 2018". Sometime later, He told me that I would have The Elephant in the Room October 2017 session. I was thinking that I'm not supposed to be in business mode. I was on break. I was taking care of me. I was doing what I wanted to do after two years of focus on school. Well, we all know how that works…it doesn't. When God gives us direction, He expects us to move in the way He is guiding us.

Needless to say, I was obedient. I trusted what He was telling me to do. I did not want to find out what the outcome would be if I didn't obey Him. During the process of planning, I confirmed a date, location, and speakers for The Elephant in the Room October session. I ordered the t-shirts for Always Wear Your Tiara and identified a location to purchase the tiaras. While I was planning, I got a text message from the bank that my account was in the negative. I was shocked and needed to find out what happened, but I couldn't get to a computer or check on my phone at the time I received the text. My account had not been in the negative for years, and I knew this was a mistake.

I began to pray and remember saying, "Lord, You told me to do these events, and it is going to require money. I need You to provide." Shortly after, I received a call from Kendra Tillman, Owner of Goodlife Diva. She wanted to be a sponsor for The Elephant in the Room October 2017, and within the same week, P.A. Patterson, Owner of Saturation Saturday Ministries called to also be a sponsor. God's provision covered the cost of the venue and food for the event. Where God leads you, He will provide.

Some people enjoy the safety of being accepted for who they are versus going through the necessary changes to become who they were designed to be. We all want to be accepted. However, some people refuse to be changed. If you're comfortable where you are, your intended purpose will not be fulfilled. Living in your purpose will require you to step out of your comfort zone. I once saw a quote that said, "If it doesn't challenge you, it won't change you." There are desires in your heart that you want to accomplish, but when it becomes challenging, you stop working on it, put it down, and walk away. You have to push yourself past the challenges. Don't wait on others to do it for you because your purpose wasn't designed for them to do it. It is for you to fulfill.

Standing in the same position is going to make it easier for others to pass you by. Then you'll be wondering why you aren't getting anywhere. Well, you didn't take off when the starting pistol was fired. You have to start running toward your goal, and you can't stop until you cross the finish line.

If you're comfortable in an area, you won't see a need to change. So you will not change. One of the areas that I am most uncomfortable in is doing

Chapter 6 | Motivation and Purpose

videos to post online or presenting in front of a camera. My friends and those I collaborate with know that when I post a video, it took everything in me to do so. In 2014, I attended a VIP retreat hosted by Dr. Nadia Brown, owner of Doyenne Leadership. We stayed at a beachfront home which was perfect for me because I absolutely love the beach. Throughout the week, I kept paying attention to the waves. I listened intently at night as the waves continued to make sound in the darkest of the night. When I woke up later in the middle of the night, the waves were still rolling. I enjoyed hearing the relaxing sounds as they filled my room. During the day when residents and vacationers were surfing, swimming, playing, boating, or jet skiing in the water, the waves never stopped. And they still haven't. Sometimes the waves were small, and sometimes they were large, yet each had a specific purpose. While the large waves excited some, others stayed at a safe distance close to the shore.

While I was at the VIP retreat, I realized that no matter what was happening in or around the water, it continued to remain within its purpose. I decided to step outside of my comfort zone and do a video related to the waves. After numerous attempts, I was finally satisfied with one that I thought was good enough to post. I gained encouragement within and said the following words on the video:

"I've been at the VIP retreat since Tuesday, and one thing I noticed is that the waves never stop fulfilling their purpose. Even when the families are not out playing in the water and when the surfers are not out, they are still fulfilling their purpose. Even when it's dark outside the waves never stop fulfilling their purpose. So I began to wonder, do we continue in our purpose even when no one is around, even in the darkness of night. When no one is there to support us or when people don't support our vision, do we continue in our purpose? I encourage you to continue to fulfill your purpose because everyone is not going to support your vision. You know what you were designed to do. So I encourage you to stay on that path of fulfilling your purpose."

I am asking you the same question that I posed on a social media site: "Are you living your purpose when you don't have support or when it gets hard and no one is watching?"

This is the year that I am going to be intentional about stepping out of that comfort zone and learn methods to increase my ability to overcome what I consider my weaknesses. I encourage you to do the same. Identify your weaknesses and be intentional about making improvements to excel beyond what you think you can't do. The more confidence you gain in your abilities, the better the outcome. Being confident and being enthusiastic about who you are and your purpose will assure others of your capabilities and strengths. You will be able to assist them through your gifts, talents, and purpose. Having a clear understanding of who you are will help you be more productive in your purpose. The most important thing in understanding yourself is that you find clarity about your purpose, and then you won't compare yourself to others as indicated in another chapter. When you understand what motivates you the most and take purposeful action steps, you feel more rewarded at the end of the day.

Chapter 6 | Motivation and Purpose

Be willing to push yourself to live in your full purpose. Acknowledge your weaknesses and learn how to excel in those areas instead of allowing a weakness to work against you.

Platforms

"What platform do you have?" I woke up one morning to this question blazing in my mind. Where did it come from? What purpose did it serve? Before I could say, "Good Morning Father", this uninvited question was invading my thoughts. The question came from a woman I was talking to after she gave a very moving speech about being a domestic violence survivor. During our conversation I mentioned to her that I also share my story of domestic violence and her response was, "What platform do you have? I'm (she told me her title), and I have a platform where I can share my story." In her opinion, if I didn't carry a specific title and wear a crown, I didn't have a platform to call myself an advocate against domestic violence. Little did she know that my tiara was at home, but I don't use it as a way to have a platform to support, empower, and encourage women.

In whatever path you are on as you move towards your purpose, don't allow naysayers to discredit you. Her words could not get a negative response out of me. I surmised that the question came back to my memory as an idea for me to encourage you to avoid allowing someone who doesn't know you to discredit and discourage you. You have a purpose that will make a difference in the lives of others regardless of whether you have a title, college degree, or crown.

In the chapter on Self-talk, you read about the importance of being aware of what you are saying to yourself. God is your biggest supporter when you are doing what He has instructed you to do. The naysayers will always be there. Avoid listening to anyone who says that you can't do something. Bypass the people who question your journey and resources. If God said to do it, it doesn't matter what others think. I am not saying that you shouldn't get the opinions of others. You will need to be able to discuss your plans and strategize with someone or a team that you trust. This is where you brainstorm and obtain valuable insight to help you. In this circle, you have people who will keep you accountable and not allow you to give up–crown or no crown.

Your gift will be an asset to others, and God gave it to you for a reason. If you find yourself making excuses for not working in your gift/purpose, you are disobeying God. If you are waiting on a specific time in your life and working on your own timeline instead of God's timeline, you are disobeying God. Delayed obedience is disobedience. You can't tap into your future by making excuses. Take necessary steps to be prepared for your future. Otherwise, don't be surprised when what you didn't do, God gifted someone else to do instead.

Imagine the number of ideas and inventions people have had, but they were afraid to take the leap. After some time, they notice that their idea and/or invention is now the success of someone else who decided to jump. You will never know how successful you can be if you don't take action. Fear of failure keeps a lot of people from doing something. I want you to at least try and if you fail, at least you are 'failing' into your future instead of remaining

Chapter 6 | Motivation and Purpose

motionless in the moment. The **fear of failure** should **never outweigh** your **potential for progress**.

Knowing what your goals are is very important. You get closer and closer to reaching your short term and even long term goals once you start completing day-to-day tasks to get there. You must show up every day with purpose in mind. As a matter of fact, don't just show up, actively show up. With this I mean show up with enthusiasm to make it your best day ever. Show up with intention in mind. Show up with an intention to succeed. Even if you thought yesterday was a great day, make today even better.

When you show up, show up on time. If you're working from home, get up, get dressed, and actively show up. Working from home does not always imply doing work for an employee. Working from home is also when you are doing things related to your business, goals, or purpose. Again, you must actively show up to be successful. This includes having a designated place to work, wearing attire that equates to working (don't hang out in your pajamas), and eliminating any distractions such as television and social media.

You can't show up late for your own production. I was speaking to someone one day after a meeting. She was telling me about how her employer expected her to arrive to work at a certain time which was actually 'on time'. There were various reasons why she wasn't arriving on time which included morning traffic, taking a different route that included construction and not having any clients until later in the day. She didn't see it necessary to arrive until it was absolutely necessary according to her needs. When asked to come in earlier than the initial time, she asked her manager if it meant that she could leave earlier than her original scheduled time. My response was that her employer had every right to expect her to be at work as scheduled and that she owed a reasonable duty to them as part of her job responsibilities. Needless to say, she did not appreciate my response.

When I asked her about her ultimate goal regarding her profession, to my surprise, she responded, "I want to own my own business." My follow-up question was about her expectancy in having her employees to show up on time. You can imagine how the conversation went from there. I was not successful in helping her understand that she needed to be the same type of employee that she would one day hope to have when she becomes a boss or employer. After this encounter, I began noticing that she became notorious for arriving late for meetings, conferences, and other outings with groups. Again I say, you can't be late for your own production. Prepare now for goals you want to achieve in the future.

What are four specific goals that you want to reach within the next six months?

1.

2.

3.

4.

What specific and purposeful action steps can you take to help reach these goals?

5.

6.

7.

8.

In order to reach your goals it is important to identify your values, capabilities, expertise, and needs. Take time to write about each one of these in regards to your purpose.

Values	Capabilities	Expertise	Needs

Identifying what you value will help you to hone in on where you can have the greatest impact. You'll also be more motivated to do the work when it holds significant value to your purpose. Knowing your capabilities allows you to have a firm foundation of your abilities, and this will give you the self-assurance you need to make the first move to reach your goals. There is something that people keep asking you about because they see you as an expert in a specific area. Whatever it is, maximize on your knowledge and expertise. This could very well be the driving force of your potential for progress to excel in your purpose. So what do you need in order to intentionally work within your purpose to inspire and be a service to others?

Having a clear grasp on what you want to achieve is important in identifying your action steps. When you don't know where you are it is difficult to get to where you want to go. Are you motivated? If not, what will it take for you to find the motivation to reach your goal? Only you can create the motivation you need to succeed. If you're waiting on others to instill motivation in you, you will be disappointed. You have to stay interested and excited about your purpose. People may encourage you, help guide you, and provide you with examples of how they are doing things, but it is up to you to do what needs to be done to reach the goal you want to accomplish. If you don't take action, your friends and family members who are encouraging you will at some point begin to realize that you're not serious and when you bring up the subject of your goals again, they may not listen with the same enthusiasm.

Chapter 6 | Motivation and Purpose

Gain some momentum. You can listen to motivational speakers and attend various conferences to obtain valuable information on how to pursue your dreams. However, once again, if you don't take action steps, it will continue to be a dream deferred. There are individuals who have obtained step-by-step instructions on how to get their invention into the hands of people who can help them become a success. Unfortunately, they didn't take action. No action = no success. They didn't believe in themselves enough to take action. They didn't seek out additional resources and support to become a success.

I have been asked, "How did you write and publish your book?" I provided them with the following list:

- I had a clear vision of what I wanted to do.

- I carved out specific times and locations to focus on writing.

- I met (actually exceeded) the weekly word count deadlines established by the editor.

- I wrote without initially focusing on grammar.

- I obtained the services of a credible and creative marketing engineer.

- I prayed and prayed some more.

- I received an idea for the book cover in a dream and communicated this to the marketing engineer.

- I read numerous articles about self-publishing.

- I asked question after question about self-publishing.

- I met with a team of women who had previously self-published.

- I saved for the revenue that was going to be needed for marketing and publishing.

After sharing my writing experience and later following up with a few of them, they hadn't started the writing process. The primary excuse has been, "I just don't have time to write." The truth of the matter is that we can all find time in our day to do at least one thing towards our purpose. You have to be attentive to the time wasters. Before you know it, an hour or two has passed because you decided to spend time on something that is irrelevant.

You have to be willing and determined to work around obstacles and make connections with others. More importantly, you must be willing to do the work. Only you can change the direction of your path to find the motivation you need to succeed.

Time Wasters

Let's take a look at some obvious time-wasters:

- social media—all platforms

- television

- talking on the phone on the ride to work, during breaks and lunch, on the ride home from work, and once you get home from work.

Chapter 6 | Motivation and Purpose

Now you may say, I can't write while driving so what's the issue with talking on the phone on the way to and from work? I received some great insight for my first book while driving. Had I been using this time to talk on the phone, I would have missed what God wanted me to hear. Your quiet time doesn't have to be in a room locked away from distractions. God is willing to speak to you whenever you make the time available to Him.

Remember in the intro when I mentioned God seeing me through to the finish line as my knee was burning halfway through the 25-mile Bike-the-Coast ride? It is the same with our purpose. When we reach those moments when it gets difficult, we have to pray and trust God throughout the entire process. While I never felt like giving up, I felt it would be difficult to complete the ride. The thoughts dissipated as I concentrated on the left knee, focused on the goal, and continued to place my trust in God.

Now it's time for focus on shifting your mindset from fear to FAITH. What do you fear the most about seeking and living out your purpose? What is holding you back? I want you to write that fear down on the line provided. Be honest with yourself so that the fears can be clearly identified, addressed, and destroyed.

_____

_____

_____

_____

Now that you've identified where you need to put faith over fear, it is now time to get up and get moving to get things done. Let's start with day-to-day activities. Looking back at your fear statement, what faith action can you take to overcome this fear?

How do you get organized for tasks that need to be completed? A friend and I have a habit of using sticky notes on our desks, refrigerators, cars and wherever we need to place one to help us be organized. Once a task is completed, we remove the sticky note. However, there are days where I have to use a Word Doc to make a list of what I need to do. This typically occurs at the beginning and end of the semester. By using the list, I don't have to go back and forth between electronic databases to identify if I had met a requirement. I simply check it off my list. Before the work-day ends, I establish goals and become organized for the next day.

Then there is the need to establish daily goals to meet my purpose. For example, when I began writing this book, my daily goal was to write four pages a day. However, life happened, and I wasn't able to write every day as planned. So what do you do when you don't meet a daily goal? Hopefully you can readjust, stay focused, and keep moving. I took a realistic look at my calendar, identified what days would be my most productive writing days, and readjusted to meet the new goal date I established with my Life Coach Crystal Blackwell, Owner of Crystal Clear Solutions. When life happens, don't get frustrated and give up. We all get off track at some point in our lives. The key is to not allow it to make you feel as if you've failed. You haven't failed. You

Chapter 6 | Motivation and Purpose

just need to shift and stay focused on the target which is your end goal.

You may want to start using a vision board to help you see what you want to accomplish. If you are a visual person like me, a vision board (or book that I do now) gives you a visual aspect of achievable goals. I used the same vision board for 2016 and 2017. I worked that vision board in 2016 because everything I had placed on it, I accomplished. I gained a healthier relationship with God, improved my eating habits by acquiring a health coach and lost 25 pounds in 6 months. I also hosted my first conference in Phoenix, saved additional money, and finished my doctoral studies with no debt. And I maintained a 4.0GPA! There is more on the vision board such as quotes and words to remind me of what I can accomplish. On the bottom right of the vision board is the following quote:

"Everyone gets ideas.
Something comes to fruition when you begin
To refine it and develop it and make it into something."
~Nelson George

In summation, you have creative ideas within you. It's time to love yourself enough to take bold steps toward your future. Don't just sit on the outside looking in while others are doing what you want to do. One person or organization cannot do everything or be everything to everybody. Perfect your gift, and walk in it as well. You must be willing to work around obstacles, make connections with others, and do the work. Only you can change the direction of your path and the direction of your thoughts to find the motivation you need to succeed. And by all means, remember that you won't be able to control the outcome of everything because you are not in control. God is! I encourage you to pray big and bold prayers, and never be afraid of what you've prayed for! Remember that in seeking your purpose to always:

Love God

Trust God

and **Love Yourself to Life!**

Chapter 6 | Closing Remarks

Closing Remarks

You may be thinking that it is difficult to **Love Yourself to Life** when you are in a broken place. The thought that you are not forgiven, lost, and surrounded by darkness are attacks of the enemy. If this is you, I encourage you to also read Broken Believer No More. In this book I share my journey from being broken to allowing God, the Ultimate Potter, to mold me into the woman He created me to be—completely loved by Him.

Made in the USA
Middletown, DE
14 October 2024